SUPPLIES

BRUSHES

Robert Simmons Series 48 #2 Fan Brush
Robert Simmons Series PH 10 Sable Flats #0, #4, #8, #10 or Langnickel Series 5280-S Royal Sable Flats #0, #4, #8, #10
Loew-Cornell's Ann's Mini Mop and Ann's Detail Mop and Scharff Series 670 Mops 1/2", 3/4", 1"
Loew-Cornell's Series 7050 Liner #1 or #0 or Langnickel Series 641 #1 or #0

PAINTS

I used oils to paint the projects in this book. However, acrylics may also be used if you prefer. You should have no trouble if you use the "floating color" and "stipple blending" techniques that are being widely taught today.

Oil Colors

Liquitex names are given below, with one exception. Specific color mixes are given in the individual project instructions.

White (Titanium Everwhite)	Ivory Black
Cadmium Yellow Medium	Cadmium Red Light
Cadmium Yellow Deep	Cadmium Red Scarlet by Shiva
Yellow Ochre	Prussian Blue
Raw Sienna	Greenish Umber (This is a dark olive green color. Sap Green with a little Burnt Umber in it will work also.)
Burnt Sienna	
Burnt Umber	
Cerulean Blue	

Acrylic Colors

If it is your preference to work in acrylics, either tube or bottled acrylics may be used. I prefer the tube acrylics because the pigment is pure and permanent. To keep them at working consistency, thin slightly and then mist the palette occasionally with water from an old window cleaner spray bottle. This should keep the paint fresh for hours. The bottled acrylics are great for backgrounds and color bands since they are already thinned to brushing consistency and are opaque enough for solid coverage in just a couple of coats.

Since I hand mix most of my colors from the standard colors available, there are no obscure color names listed in the oil color list and your local art supply store or tole shop should be able to help you choose the corresponding acrylic colors needed.

PUNCH SUPPLIES

The Tandy Leather Company has graciously consented to make the tools I used for these projects available to the tole industry so you will be able to get them thru your local craft or tole shop. If you are not able to find them you may write Tandy directly at the address listed on page 31. They will be happy to send you their mail order catalog which has a complete listing of their nationwide chain of retail stores.

Tin punching awl for a starter punch—available at your local craft shop
Tandy Wood Punch Tool Set
  or, you may wish to obtain its contents separately: Tandy Craftools #S931, #S932 and #A99
  Small wood or rawhide mallet

OTHER SUPPLIES

Disposable waxed palette
Palette knife
Odorless paint thinner
Linseed oil
Round synthetic sponge for sponging background gesso on some pieces. I purchase mine from my local ceramic shop.
Soft, lint free rags—for brush wiping and staining; your husband's T-shirts are ideal.
Tracing paper
Scissors
Chalk
Pencil
Tracing stylus for tracing patterns and antiquing punchwork
Sandpaper—fine grit regular and #400 wet-dry
Wood filler
Tack rag
Varnish—I used McCloskey's Heirloom Varnish Eggshell Finish for these projects but a good water base varnish may be used also.
Wood Sealer—I used McCloskey's Clear Wood Sealer #2931 and recommend it for best results, however the water base varnish may be used also.
Odorless brush cleaning fluid
Brush cleaning oil (I use Better Way Brush Oil)
Liquitex Acrylic Gesso
Painting Medium
  For oils—Make a portion of "half and half" by pouring equal amounts of paint thinner and linseed oil into a small jar. Pour amounts into a jar lid as needed.
  For Acrylics—Use Matte Medium by Liquitex or water base varnish. By using medium with your acrylic paints you will be sealing each successive layer of paint that you apply in shading your design. This will prevent the paint that is underneath from rinsing off when you apply the next color on top of it.
Several small jars—for storing paint thinner, "half and half", rinse water, etc.

PROJECT PREP AND FINISHING

SPONGING TECHNIQUES

I keep a separate small jar of tinted gesso on hand. Pour out a small jar of gesso, add a squirt or two of Delta Ceramcoat Straw acrylic and mix. The gesso is tinted only very sparingly to an off-white color. This will become the highlight color when painting so it shouldn't be very dark.

Pour a puddle of tinted gesso onto your palette or into the jar lid. Using a sponge of the appropriate size (cut your sponge in half and then one of the halves in half), dip into the gesso and begin sponging with an up and down motion. Keep sponging until you have an overall, even coverage and texture.

The sponge will give you an even, pebbly texture, something like fabric. The pebbles should not be too large or your liner work will look uneven. Do not saturate the sponge with gesso or you won't be able to get a nice, small, even texture. Sand lightly between coats of gesso. Three coats are usually needed. Allow the last coat to dry for several hours if possible before decorating the project.

TRANSFERRING PATTERNS

When tracing the punchwork designs, be careful to do an accurate tracing so that the spaces between dots are as even as possible and that the wheat shapes are angled towards the stems in a uniform manner. When tracing the painting patterns, it is only necessary to trace the basics, not every dot, stitch, or liner stroke.

Rub on the back of the tracing with a soft pencil when transferring to light backgrounds and rub with chalk for medium to dark backgrounds.

Line up pattern on piece and tape down. Re-trace pattern using a stylus or "dead" ballpoint pen. When transferring to the sponged gesso backgrounds, press only very lightly so that you do not leave dark, smeary lines that will smudge and discolor your paint or be hard to cover up.

VARNISHING

Make sure the piece is completely dry. Use a tack rag and wipe the piece thoroughly to remove dust bunnies and foreign matter. Never shake your container of varnish—always stir it carefully with a spoon.

Try to avoid a high humidity day to varnish. Your coats of varnish will dry faster without clouding. Your varnish and your project should be at room temperature. I use a sponge brush to apply oil base varnish and a Grumbacher Aquarelle Series 6142 to apply water base varnish.

Varnish should be applied in thin even coats. Avoid brushing back over areas you have already coated unless you have a bad run or drip. This can lead to a gooey mess.

After the second coat of varnish is thoroughly dry, use the #400 wet—dry sandpaper to lightly sand the entire piece. Use it dry unless you have a drip or run to sand down. Wipe with the tack rag.

Three coats of varnish are sufficient for oil base varnish but you will need more coats if using water base varnish. I usually apply six.

WOOD PUNCHING– BASIC STEPS

Our early American ancestors used simple tools to decorate their handmade furniture and it is that feeling that I have tried to capture with the designs for this book. Many of the designs are reminiscent of those used for the tin punch crafts and could certainly be interchanged with those in the many design books available.

It is a good idea to do the following procedures on some scrap wood to get the feel for the mallet and tools and to experiment with punch depth and rhythm. Do not be too concerned with a few splits and "munchies" in the wood as you work. The finishing procedures will compensate for a great deal. There are a few plain punch practice patterns on the following pages to use for beginning projects. Note, also, the Wood Punch Worksheet on page 8.

1. Make a careful tracing of the punch pattern and transfer the design as carefully as possible.

2. For round punch shapes, hold the tin punch awl vertically against wood and start each hole with a few light taps of the mallet on the awl handle. This prevents splitting when the more blunt tools are used. Next, switch to the #S931 and enlarge the holes with a few light taps. If a larger size hole is specified on the pattern, you will then do the procedure again using the #S932. By enlarging the hole gradually, you can prevent splitting and crushing the wood. The smooth tapered sides and rounded ends of the Tandy Craftools make a smooth, tapered hole which will form a neat "well" for the antiquing to be applied later.

3. The wheat punch impression is done in one step. Place the tool vertically on the piece and rock gently back and forth as you tap with the mallet so that you are making the impression gradually. This helps prevent splitting.

4. After the punchwork is completed, re-sand the entire piece to work out the worst of the splits and "munchies". I use my electric sander for this. Dust out the punchwork with a clean, large, dry brush. A 1" house painting trim brush works well for this.

5. Reinforce the punchwork where needed by going over the piece again with mallet and punches to deepen any impressions that might have been sanded too shallow.

6. Seal the piece by applying a coat of McCloskey's #2931 Clear Wood Sealer. Brush the sealer well into the punchwork in order to flood the dents and holes with the fluid. This seals the areas of end grain that are exposed in the holes when the piece is punched and prevents the antiquing from bleeding and running under the surface of the wood producing unsightly streaks and spoiling the design. **This is a key step in the procedure.**

If you are doing a piece that calls for a little scene to be painted on raw wood, you must postpone this step till after your scene is done and dry. The sealer is then applied carefully around (not on top of) the scene and on the rest of the piece.

If not painting a raw wood scene, go ahead and decorate the piece after the sealer is dry using the procedures outlined in the individual project instructions.

7. Since the amber color of the wood sealer tones the wood to the natural golden color that is so popular in wood finishing today, the samples for the projects in this book were not actually stained but rather antiqued on the edges using the following procedures:

ANTIQUING WOOD

Brush a coat of "half and half" on the entire piece and wipe gently with a soft cloth leaving the surface a little damp. Fold a piece of soft lint-free cloth around your index finger and touch into your jar lid of "half and half". Blot well on a paper towel and pass your cloth-wrapped finger across the open end of a tube of Burnt Umber oil paint, picking up a little color. Now, using a circular motion, apply the stain to the edges of the areas you are antiquing. Blend the paint on the damp surface until you gain the effect you desire. You will need to turn to a clean area of your cloth from time to time for the blending procedure. If you get the stain too dark, rinse off with "half and half", if too light, go over the piece again using more paint. This takes a little practice to get used to but is much faster than traditional antiquing methods. It is also less messy. Allow the stain to dry overnight.

---

8. Apply two coats of varnish, allowing the piece to dry thoroughly between coats. Be sure to flood the punchwork with varnish each time. This creates little sealed "wells" for the antiquing. After the second coat is dry, lightly sand the entire piece with #400 wet-dry sandpaper.

9. There are two methods to antique the punchwork. First, you may follow standard antiquing procedures by mixing Burnt Umber (or color of choice) and "half and half" or use a pre-mixed antiquing "mud" and brush over the entire piece, flooding the punchwork well. Allow the antiquing to set up and wipe the excess off with a soft cloth. Stubborn areas are removed with a 3M scrubbie or steel wool dampened in paint thinner. Allow to dry overnight before the final coat of varnish. The second method is the one I use:

ANTIQUING PUNCHWORK

Pour a bit of Delta Ceramcoat Burnt Umber onto your palette and add a couple of drops of water. Using the tracing stylus, place a drop of paint into each punch hole. When doing the wheat punches, spread the drop of paint to neatly fill each dent. This may seem like a lot of work and not very traditional but it is actually faster. There is no waiting time for the antiquing to set up before wiping down, no messy wiping and scrubbing, and no overnight wait before final varnishing. It is also more accurate.

---

10. After the antiquing is dry, apply the final coat of varnish.

SPECIAL PAINTING TECHNIQUES

RAW WOOD SCENES

This method of painting has been used in decorative painting for years but I will outline some tips and suggestions that have been helpful for me. The main thing to remember when painting on raw wood is that it is rather like painting on a sponge. Therefore it is necessary to dampen each area with "half and half" as you paint to set up the wood with moisture so that it doesn't grab the paint too fast and create a blotchy mess.

Skies. Dampen the entire sky area with "half and half". Apply a coat of White that has been thinned to a creamy consistency. Now add the blue mix (described in individual instructions) at the top of the sky area and blend and fade down toward the horizon. The sky should be a darker value at the top and then fade to very light behind the background trees. Drybrush on a very sparing amount of the additional sky colors listed in individual projects. The clouds are pounced on with a large, old, worn out sable brush and their bottoms are softened into the sky with a clean, dry brush or your finger.

6

Foliage. The first color in each foliage list is applied with the corner of an old, worn out sable flat that has been dampened with "half and half" and blotted on your wiping cloth. No old, worn out brushes? Not to worry. Use a scumbling brush instead. But just as soon as you have an old worn out brush you can switch. I think you will find that they work best. Continue to work your way down the color list tapping the foliage on using scant amounts of dry paint on that old brush.

Fence Posts and Tree Trunks. Burnt Umber is thinned with "half and half" and applied with the liner. White is streaked on the highlight sides of posts, etc. with the liner.

Barns. First dampen the barn sides with "half and half". Streak shading color specified down from the eaves with the chisel edge of a small flat sable. Again, using the chisel edge of your flat, streak on the base color specified stroking in both upward and downward directions. Apply the highlights in the same manner. Dampen the roof areas with "half and half" and the base color specified. Shading colors are drybrushed on with the flat as are the highlights. Work in the direction the roof slants. Details and edges are sharpened with Burnt Umber and the liner brush.

Grass. Grass areas are first washed with "half and half" alone, then a wash of "half and half" plus the base color specified is applied. Drybrush on the shading colors specified with your flat sable in a horizontal streaking manner. Light colored grassy bunches are tapped on with an old fan brush in the order specified.

Water. Dampen the water section with "half and half". Apply creamy consistency white over all. Using a dry brush, streak with the sky blue mix and then the accent colors specified. Pull the bank shading çolors down from the water's edges streaking into the water. Soften the shading with a small mop brush, dusting back and forth in a horizontal direction.

Roads. Dampen the road area with "half and half". Wash over the road with the base color specified plus "half and half" and streak on the shading colors with a dry brush. Do the same with the highlight colors.

Glazing Finishing Tints. After the painting is dry, continuity of color and general mood can be added to the painting by glazing small amounts of color on here and there. Apply a small amount of "half and half" where specified and mop over the area. Apply a small amount of thinned paint in the suggested color with a flat brush and re-mop for a very soft, subtle effect.

QUILTED APPLIQUE

On Sealed Wood. Apply very small amounts of almost dry paint. Start with the base color specified and scrub to the edges of the pattern lines with an old worn out brush. The shading color is applied next in the same manner. Highlights are pounced on the highlight areas with somewhat thicker amounts of dry paint on a small, dry, old, worn out sable flat. Use a very light touch for applying the highlights. Stitches and decorations are added after the base areas are dry.

On Gessoed Backgrounds. The base colors specified are applied with an appropriate sized flat that has been dipped in "half and half", blotted and side loaded with color. Mop each area to soften the shading. The sponged gesso becomes the highlight. Details are added with the liner after base areas are dry.

HOME SWEET HOME

Gary designed this piece for the needle artist to use as a unique frame for "fancy work" so, not to be outdone, I transformed one of my most popular designs into a needlework type pattern. This little fat bird has a "Home Sweet Home" on her nest and I hope she finds a place in your home too.

PREPARATION. Use the S931 then the S932 for the dots on the pattern. Use the A99 for the flower petals and leaves. Don't forget to turn the punch in the proper direction for petal or leaf as you punch. Seal the frame board and sand. Stain the edges of the frame with Burnt Umber. Sponge three even coats of tinted gesso on the heart panel.

COLORS

White	Burnt Umber
Yellow Ochre	Black
Cadmium Yellow Medium	Cerulean Blue
Cadmium Yellow Light	Cadmium Red Light
Burnt Sienna	

PROCEDURE. This technique is very transparent, with the exception of the bird and blossom centers. All highlights are the base coat of gesso.

1. Wash a thin coat of YO on the branches and nests. Shade with BS, then BU. Work around the highlight areas. If you cover your highlight areas too heavily with your shading colors, simply wipe out some highlights with a damp brush and softly mop over all.

2. The leaves are washed in with a light leaf green made with YO, CYL and Black. They are shaded with dark leaf green (light leaf green plus more Black).

3. The blossoms are washed on with light pink made with CRL plus BS plus White. They are shaded with CRL plus BS. Reinforce the shading in the darkest areas with BS. The blossom centers are CYM, shaded with BS and highlighted with White. Tiny freckles around the outside edges of centers are BU.

4. The bird has a Cerulean head and body that is highlighted with White. She has a light pink cheek and tummy that are both highlighted with White. There is Cerulean detailing on her wing and tail. Her eye is Black highlighted with White. Her beak is CYM outlined with BS. She has three little topknot strokes made with a liner brush double loaded with White and Cerulean.

5. All liner work on the branches, leaves, blossoms, and tendrils are BU. The triple dot cluster fillers are made with a medium pink and the single dot fillers are Cerulean plus White.

6. After the piece is dry, brush a light coat of "half and half" on the entire surface and glaze the outside edges with Yellow Ochre. Use the mop brush to pull and soften the glaze for an antiqued look. Wipe the glaze off the bird, blossoms, branches, nest and leaves.

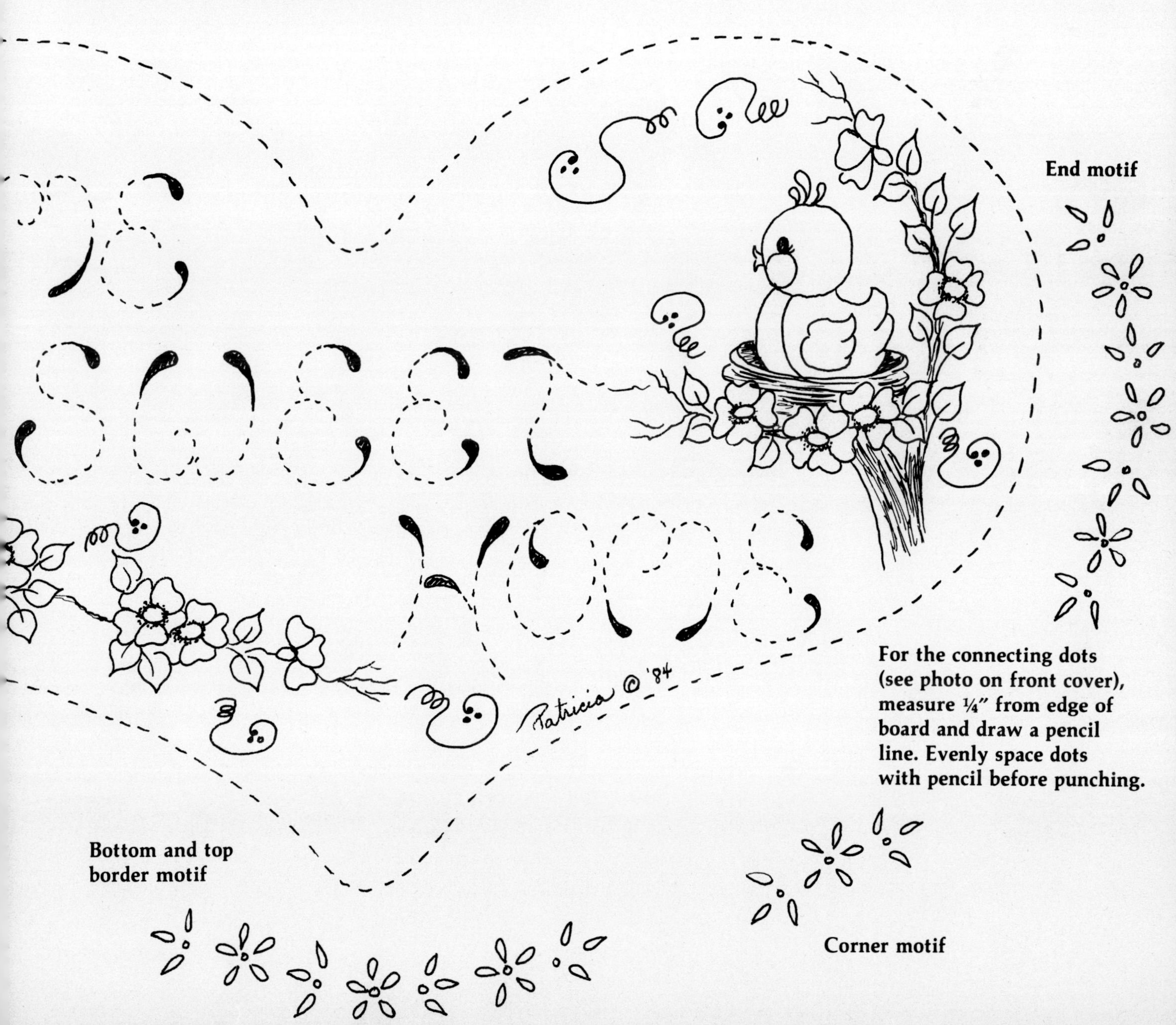

End motif

For the connecting dots (see photo on front cover), measure ¼" from edge of board and draw a pencil line. Evenly space dots with pencil before punching.

Bottom and top border motif

Corner motif

WOOD PUNCH WORKSHEET

Punch and seal

Stain

Antique punchwork

Completed motif of applique on sealed wood

Block in colors and rub with a soft cloth

Antique punchwork

Base washes

Add shading

Highlight and detail

Baby Photo Album border motif—measure ¼"
in from edges of the album and draw pencil line.
Measure off ½" intervals and make your pattern
for the border.

BABY PHOTO ALBUM

This piece would make a lovely shower gift for a new arrival. I painted it for a girl but with a color change or two, it could be for a boy also.

PREPARATION. Use the S931 to punch the tatted borders around the oval inset and album edges. Seal the piece and sand. Stain the edges of all pieces of the album. Sponge three coats of tinted gesso on the oval inset. Seal little Teddy Love and sponge three coats of tinted gesso on the little heart he is holding.

COLORS

White	Burnt Umber
Cadmium Yellow Medium	Black
Cadmium Red Light	Yellow Ochre
Burnt Sienna	

PROCEDURE

1. Make a medium pink mix using CRL, BS and White. Dampen the oval inset with "half and half" and, using a large brush sideloaded with the pink, float the color around the outside edge of the oval. Use a large mop brush to pull and soften the pink towards the middle of the inset. Work till you have a smooth blend from light to dark. Allow this to dry.

2. Paint a coat of "half and half" on each section of the teddy before adding color. Float BU on each section using the photo as a guide for shading placement. After floating color on a section, use your finger wrapped in a soft cloth to soften the edges of color.

3. Teddy's heart is washed with "half and half" and then shaded with a bit darker pink than that used for the oval inset. The teddy's cheeks are shaded with this same darker pink.

4. The leaves and blossoms above and below the oval inset are painted in the same colors and techniques as those for the Home Sweet Home hanger board. Allow all pieces to dry before doing the trim work.

5. All liner work and stitches are done in Burnt Umber. The oval inset has triple dot clusters of a light cream mix made with White plus a tad of YO. Teddy's heart has checks of the dark pink mix. Teddy himself has Black eyes that are highlighted with White. He has two little White highlight strokes on his cheeks.

6. After the final varnish coat is dry, use rust grosgrain ribbon for the hinge on the album. Use light pink ribbon for ties and use narrow rust ribbon to fashion a tiny bow around Teddy's neck before you glue him onto the oval inset.

MALLARD DECOY

This is an elegant piece that does not require much work at all. It would be prized by any man who received it I am sure.

PREPARATION. Use the S931 then the S932 to make the dot punches and the A99 for the wheat motifs. Be sure to wedge this little ducky well against something as you work because his little rounded body wiggles around as you work. Seal the piece and sand lightly.

COLORS

White	Greenish Umber
Burnt Umber	Cadmium Red Scarlet
Cadmium Yellow Medium	Burnt Sienna

PROCEDURE. This is basically a glorified staining job only you use more colors. Refer to the instructions for staining the pieces in the wood punch section and use the Greenish Umber for the head, the Cad. Yellow Medium for the bill, Cad. Red Scarlet plus Burnt Sienna for the chest and Burnt Umber for the remainder of the body. Use Burnt Umber to blend and erase lines between the color sections in order to achieve a gradual transition between sections. Refer to the photo of the finished piece for exact color placement. Use thinned White on your liner to paint the ring around his neck. Dry. Paint the wheat stems with Burnt Umber on your liner. Keep it light.

COOKIE BOX

PREPARATION. Use the S931 for the dots on the punch pattern. Use the A99 for the hearts, tulips and leaves. Don't forget to turn the punch in the proper direction for tulip, leaf or heart formation. Seal the lid and box and allow to dry before staining with Burnt Umber. The heart shaped panel is painted raw wood style so it only needs to be sanded.

COLORS

White	Burnt Sienna
Cadmium Yellow Medium	Burnt Umber
Yellow Ochre	Black
Cadmium Red Light	Cerulean Blue

PROCEDURE. Refer to the general instructions for painting the raw wood scenes.

1. The sky is Cerulean plus White drybrushed with YO then light pink (CRL plus BS plus White). Add a few fluffy White clouds.

2. The trees are light leaf green (YO plus CYM plus Black). Next use BU, then YO plus CYM, and finally light pink. The foreground bushes and tree foliage are the same.

Continued on page 12

COLOR WORKSHEET

Applique on sponged gesso background

Block in colors

Blend

Detail after dry

Base colors   **Shade**   **Detail**

Float on shading on each area and blend one at a time

Detail

3. The barn is shaded with BU and based with CRL plus a tad of BS. The highlights are White plus CYM and White plus sky blue. Windows and doors are BU with White trim. The roof areas are washed with YO and shaded with BS, then BU. The edges of the roof are highlighted with White plus sky blue.

4. The grass is washed with YO, shaded BU then BS and fluffed with light green, then CYM plus YO, then White plus CYM plus YO. Add a few fluffs of light pink to suggest flowers.

5. The swing is BU highlighted with White as is the tree trunk.

STRAWBERRY CRATE

PREPARATION. Use the S931, then the S932 for the dots and the A99 for the hearts to punch the border for the insets on both ends of the crate. Seal the piece and after it is dry, apply three coats of tinted gesso on the insets with a sponge. Stain the crate and allow to dry.

COLORS

Cadmium Yellow Medium Cadmium Red Light
Yellow Ochre Cadmium Red Scarlet
Cadmium Orange Burnt Umber
Black

This little crate is a really lovely size to be used to pack a gift of some home canned goodies for a special friend.

MIXES

1. Equal parts Cadmium Yellow Medium and Yellow Ochre plus a tad of Black (leaf green).
2. Cadmium Orange plus a tad of Cadmium Red Light.
3. Cadmium Red Scarlet plus a tad of Cadmium Red Light.

PROCEDURE. Refer to the general instructions for Quilted Applique on Gessoed Backgrounds and paint as follows:

1. Leaves are #1 mix. Strawberries are #2 mix shaded with #3 mix.

2. After the base washes are dry, dampen the entire inset with "half and half" and float Yellow Ochre around the edges. Use a large mop brush to soften this glaze and fade it out towards the center of the inset. Wipe the glaze off of the individual sections of the design so the highlights are cleared. Allow this to dry.

3. The stitches, liner work and fill in strokes are Burnt Umber. The strawberries have checks of #3 mix. The berry leaves are spattered with Burnt Umber acrylic for a homespun effect.

COVERED SCOOP

This piece would be lovely with an arrangement of dried flowers in it. Follow the general instructions for the punchwork and use the S931 then the S932 for the dots and the A99 tool for the wheat designs. The little scene is painted exactly the same way in the same colors as the scene for the Scalloped Plate. The rickrack and wheat stems are done with BU on your liner.

SCALLOPED PLATE

PREPARATION. Use the S931 then the S932 for the dots on the punch pattern. Use the A99 for the wheat patterns. Since this piece is painted in the raw wood style you will not seal the plate until the scene is painted and has dried.

COLORS

White
Cadmium Yellow Medium
Yellow Ochre
Cadmium Yellow Deep
Cadmium Red Light
Burnt Sienna
Burnt Umber
Black
Cerulean Blue

Divide the plate rim into 6 equal parts and repeat this motif

PROCEDURE. Refer to the general instructions for painting the raw wood scenes.

1. The sky is Cerulean plus White faded to almost White at the horizon. Drybrush a little CYD and some BS into the sky above the horizon. Add some fluffy clouds of White.

2. The background trees and those behind the barn are based in light green made with CYM plus YO plus tads of BU and Black. Next, use BS then BU and finally sprinkle on a few leaves of CYD. Add tiny little branches with BU on your liner.

3. All of the grass is first washed in with YO then shaded with BS then BU. Add fluffy highlights of White plus YO plus CYM, and White plus CYD.

4. The barn is shaded with BU and based with CRL plus a tad of BS. The highlights are White plus CYM and White plus CYD. The roof sections are washed with YO and scruffed with BS then BU. The roof edges are highlighted with White. Doors and windows are BU with White trim.

GUN RACK

Gary loves to build black powder guns. He has a Pennsylvania flint lock rifle for which he designed this hanger board so that we may display it on the wall.

PREPARATION. Use the S931 then the S932 for the dots in the punch design. Use the A99 for the wheat patterns. Seal the board and stain the edges with Burnt Umber. The panel is painted raw wood style so it only needs to be sanded before you begin.

COLORS

White	Raw Sienna
Cadmium Yellow Medium	Burnt Sienna
Yellow Ochre	Burnt Umber
Cadmium Yellow Deep	Black
Ultramarine Blue	

5. The pond is first based in with White. The banks on the far side are shaded with BU and BS. Drybrush Cerulean on the foreground of the pond and a little CYD and YO goes in the center. Drybrush a little CRL plus BS next to the back bank for a reflection of the barn.

6. The foreground trees have trunks of BU and barky highlights of White. The foliage is BS then BU. Add a few light foliage dabs of YO. Dab on some low bushes and pull up some foreground grass with the liner.

PROCEDURE. Refer to the general instructions for painting the raw wood scenes.

1. Make a smoky blue for the sky with White plus UB plus a tad of BU. Drybrush a little CYD up into the sky above the horizon. Add very soft puffy clouds with White.

2. Base the background trees with RS. Next, use BS then BU. Add a few highlights with CYD and CYM plus White.

3. The barn is shaded with BU and based with RS. Add highights of White plus CYM and White plus sky blue. Doors and windows are BU trimmed with White. The roofs are washed with YO, streaked with BS then BU and highlighted with White plus sky blue.

4. The grass is washed with RS. Scruff BS then BU for shading. Grassy tufts are fluffed on with RS, CYM plus YO, White plus CYM and White plus CYD. Add a few fluffs of White plus sky blue.

5. The road is washed with RS, shaded with BU and highlighted with White plus CYM.

6. Tree trunks and fence posts are BU highlighted with White. Fence wire is Black.

7. All foreground bushes and tree foliage are done in the same colors as the background trees leaning towards the darker values more heavily.

8. After the scene is dry, glaze a little warm peachy glow above the horizon with CYD then BS. Make a smoky grey brown with Black plus BU and pat over the background trees here and there. Glaze some UB plus BU on the barn roof and in the shadow areas of the road.

9. Paint the wheat stems and scallops on the acorn tops with BU on the liner brush.

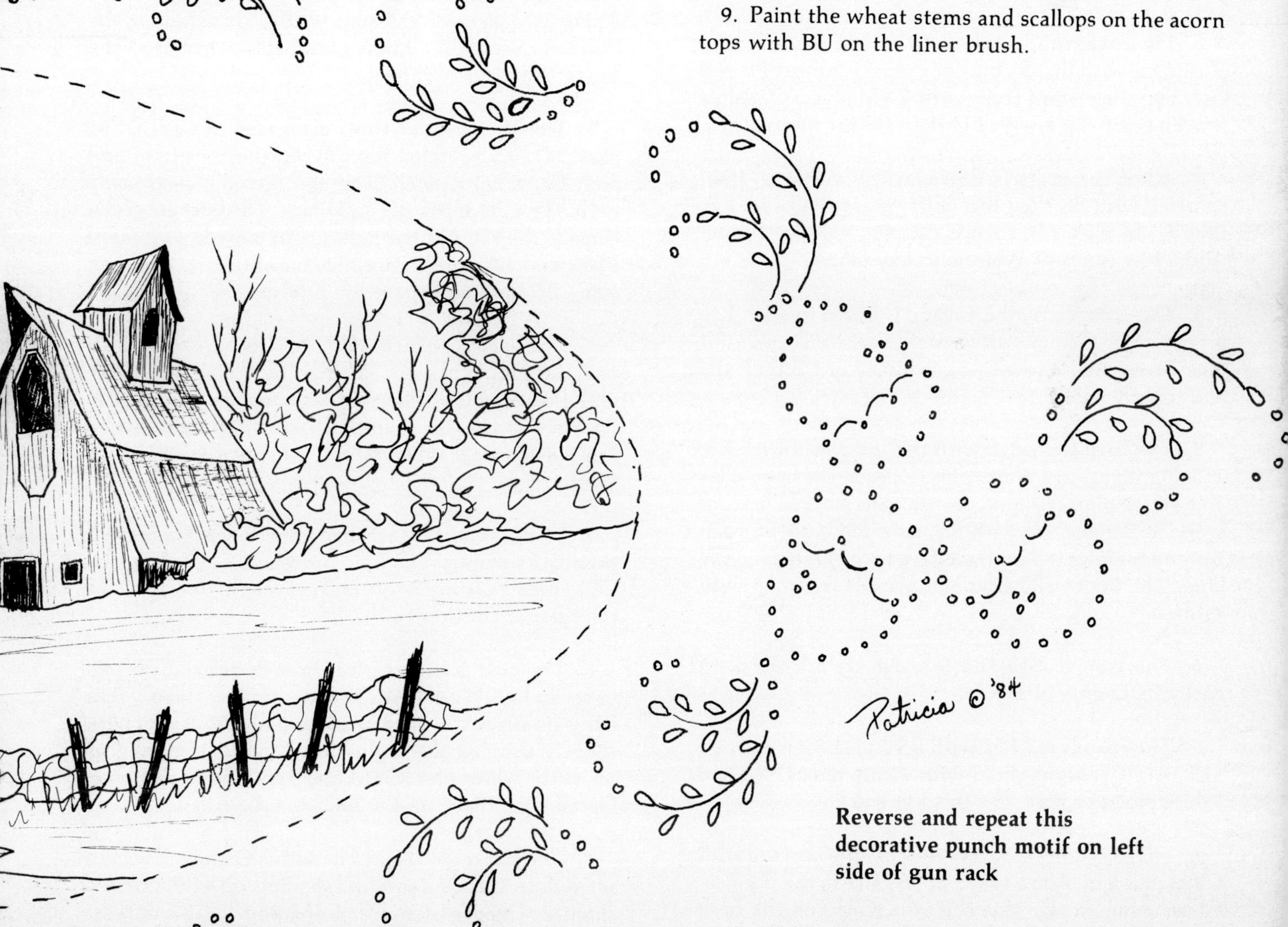

Reverse and repeat this decorative punch motif on left side of gun rack

FIRESIDE STOOL

PREPARATION. Use the S931 tool to punch the designs on the entire stool. Since the scene is painted raw wood style, you will wait to seal the piece till the scene is painted and has dried.

COLORS

White	Burnt Sienna
Cadmium Yellow Medium	Burnt Umber
Yellow Ochre	Prussian Blue
Raw Sienna	Black
Greenish Umber	

PROCEDURE. Refer to the general instructions for painting the raw wood scenes.

1. The sky blue mix is White plus PB plus a tad of BU to tone. Drybrush a bit of CYM plus YO at the horizon. Make some very soft fluffy White clouds. Mop over the entire sky to soften the clouds.

2. The background trees are based with a smoky blue made with the sky blue mix plus tads more PB and GU. Top the distant trees with CYM plus YO. Add a few bits of foliage with BU then BS for interest.

3. All of the grass is first washed with YO, then scruffed with BS then BU. Fluffy grass colors are RS, then CYM plus YO, then CYM plus YO plus White. Add a few fluffs of White plus sky blue.

4. The balance of the foliage is based in with RS. Next, apply a smoky green made with GU plus PB plus Black. Add a few foliage clumps of BS then BU and top off with a few highlights of YO.

5. The barn is shaded with BU and based with RS. The highlights are White plus CYM on the light sides and White plus sky blue on the dark sides. The roof sections are washed with RS, scruffed with BS then BU and highlighted on the edges with White plus sky blue. The doors and windows are BU trimmed with White.

6. The tree trunks and fence posts are BU with barky highlights of White.

7. The road is washed with RS and shaded with BS and BU. It is highlighted with White plus CYM and White plus sky blue. Let the scene dry.

8. Glaze a sunny glow in the sky at the horizon with CYM plus YO. Add a touch of BS glaze in the sky also. Glaze some smoky blue (PB plus Black) on the barn roof in the shadow areas and in the shadows of the road also. Let the scene dry before proceeding with the finishing steps.

TRIPLE FRAME BOARD

PREPARATION. Punch the side panels with the S931 punch tool. Seal the punched panels and stain their edges and the frame with Burnt Umber. The center panel is painted raw wood style so it only needs to be sanded well before you begin.

COLORS

White	Prussian Blue
Cadmium Yellow Medium	Burnt Sienna
Yellow Ochre	Burnt Umber
Raw Sienna	Black

PROCEDURE. Refer to the general instructions for painting the raw wood scenes.

1. The sky blue mix is PB plus a tad of BU to tone, mixed into a little White to make a medium blue. There is a little CYM plus YO drybrushed at the horizon to suggest a sunny glow behind the trees. The fluffy clouds are White.

2. The background trees are based in with CYM plus YO. RS is added next. Keep the tops light and airy. Use a light touch. The light green is next made with YO, CYM, BS, BU and Black. The darkest green is made the same as the light green but add a bit more Black and a tad of PB. Sprinkle on a little BU and then some BS here and there for interest.

3. The barn is shaded with BU. The base color is RS and the highlights are White plus CYM and White plus the sky blue. The roof sections are YO washes with streaks of BS then BU. White highlights go all around the edges. Doors and windows are BU with White trim.

4. The grass is first washed in with RS. There is BS then BU shading. The light tufts are CYM plus YO, CYM plus YO plus White and a few light blue ones for the sake of continuity.

5. The post is first washed in with YO and allowed to set awhile. Wash in the shadow areas with very thin BU plus Black. Deepen shading and add cracks with slightly thinned Black plus BU. Drybrush highlights on with White plus CYM and White plus sky blue. Detail with Black on the liner brush.

6. The bucket is washed in with YO and allowed to set awhile. Dab on dents and shading with BS, thinned slightly. Deepen dents and shading in the darkest areas with slightly thinned BU. Detail with BU plus Black on the liner and highlight with White plus CYM. The bucket bail is black highlighted with White and the handle is done the same as the fence post.

Continued on page 23

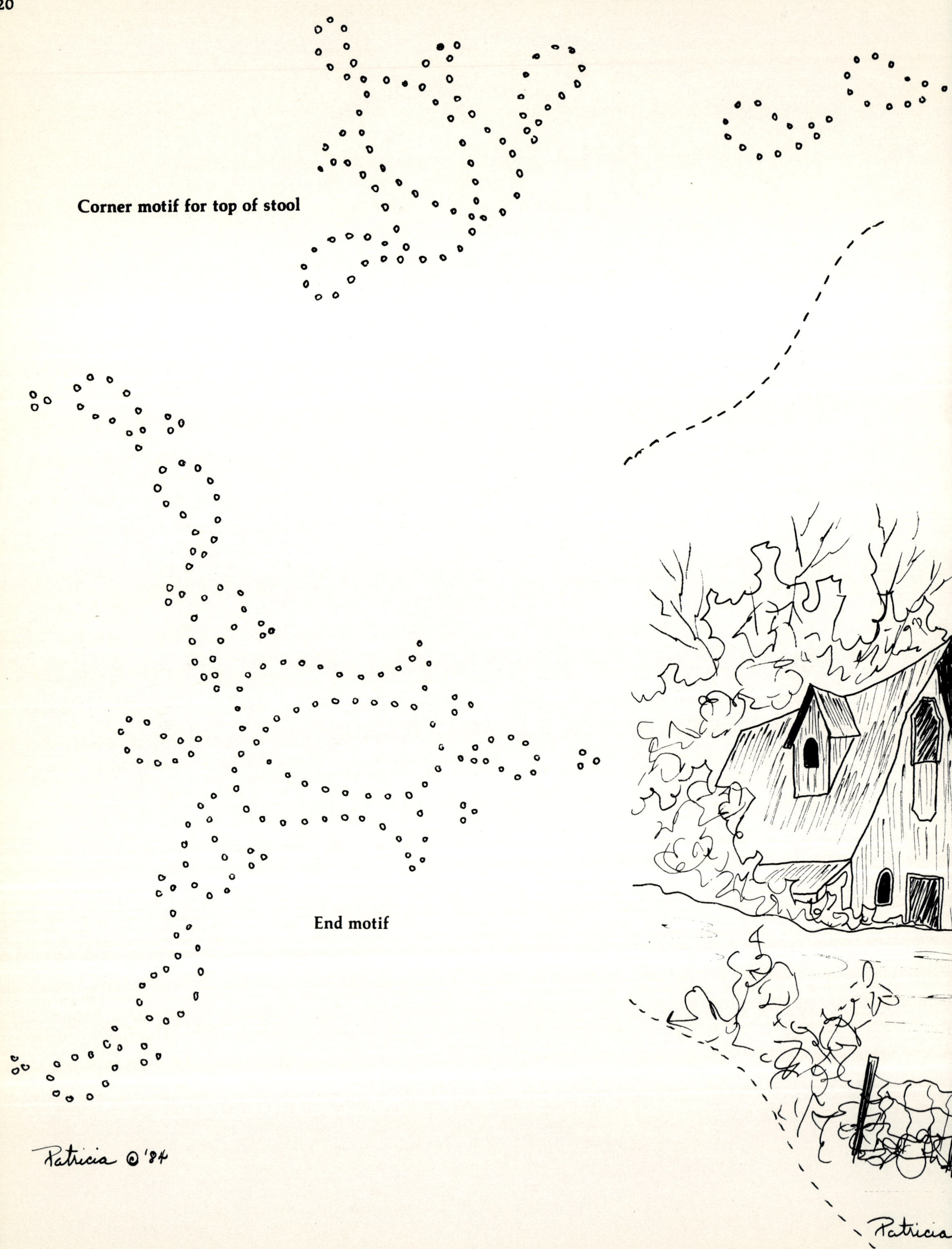

Corner motif for top of stool

End motif

Patricia ©'84

FIRESIDE STOOL

SEAN

TRIPLE FRAME

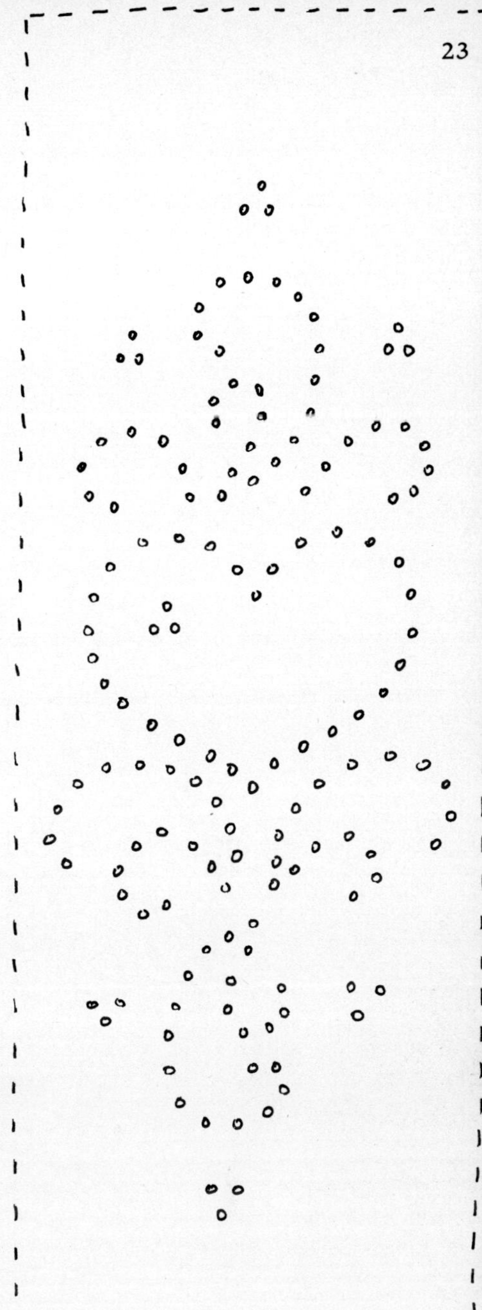

Patricia © '84

7. Tree foliage in the upper left corner is made with the dark green. Add some BU for interest and sprinkle a little YO plus CYM on the sunny ends of the branches.

8. The bushes around the post are the same colors as those in the background trees only stay with the darker values this time. The road is washed with RS, shaded with BU and highlighted with White plus CYM.

9. Pull some tiny branches of BU out from the foliage in all areas. The fence wire is Black. Allow scene to dry. Glaze a little sky blue in the shadow areas of the road, roof and bucket. Glaze a warm sunny glow over the tree tops at the horizon with CYM plus YO.

BREAD BOX

PREPARATION. Use the S931 then the S932 to punch the apple and leaf designs. Seal the entire bread box and lid. Stain the pieces with BU. The panel is painted raw wood style so only a good sanding is needed.

COLORS

White	Burnt Sienna
Yellow Ochre	Burnt Umber
Cadmium Yellow Medium	Black
Raw Sienna	Cadmium Red Scarlet
Prussian Blue	Cadmium Red Light

Continued on page 25

Top center motif

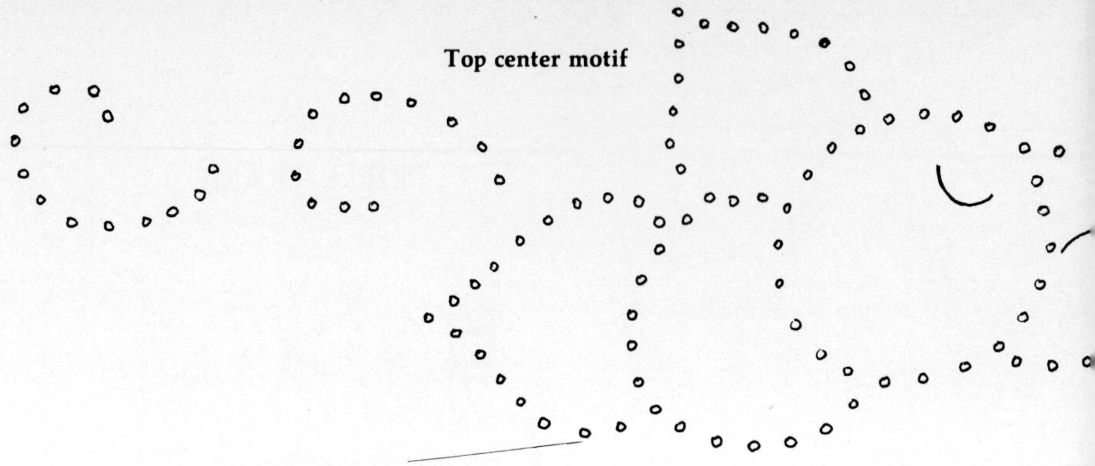

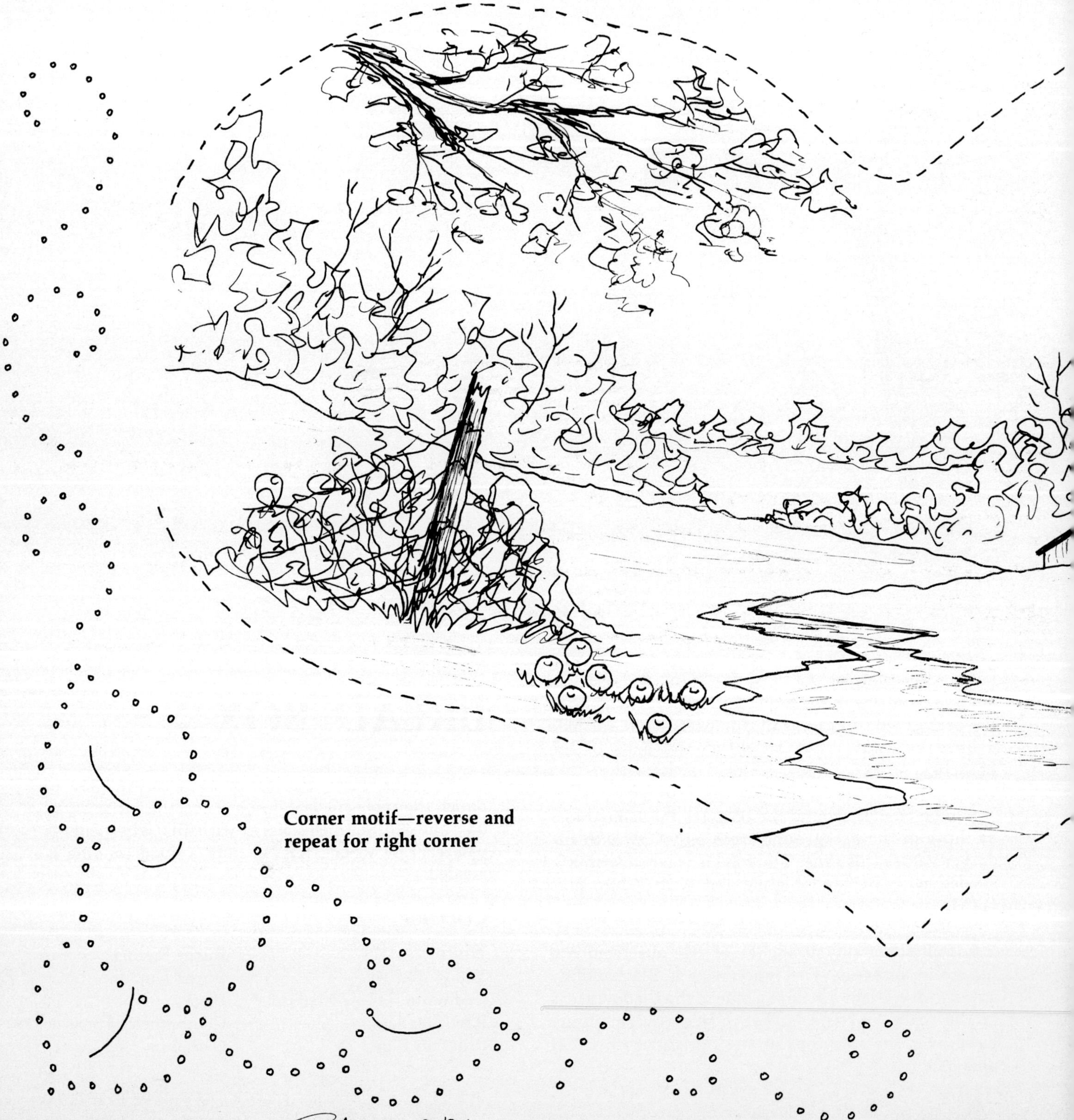

Corner motif—reverse and repeat for right corner

Patricia © '84

BREADBOX

Patricia © '84

Gary designed this slant lid bread box many years ago and it has been very popular. It is very large and holds three of the long loaves of bread as well as other goodies. For the theme of this book, however, he cut a heart out of the center of the lid and inserted a birch plywood panel. The plywood panel could be removed and replaced with a tin punched panel if you prefer.

PROCEDURE. Refer to the general instructions for painting the raw wood scenes.

1. The entire scene with the exception of the foreground apples is done in the same colors and techniques as the one in the triple frame board.

2. The apples are based in CRL and shaded with CRS plus BU. They are highlighted with CYM then White.

3. The punched apples and leaves are not really painted with a brush but rather the paint is rubbed on with your finger wrapped in a soft cloth. The leaves are leaf green shaded with BU and highlighted with CYM. The apples are CRL shaded with CRS plus BU and highlighted with White plus CYM. The leaf veins are made with a very faint liner stroke of BU.

ROCKING HORSE PLAQUE

PREPARATION. Use the S931 to punch the design on the rocker section. Seal, stain, varnish and antique. The pony gets three coats of tinted gesso sponged on him before painting.

COLORS

White	Burnt Sienna
Cadmium Red Scarlet	Burnt Umber
Raw Sienna	Cerulean Blue
Black	

PROCEDURE

1. Dampen the pony head, body, and legs a section at a time with half and half and float Cerulean on the shaded areas. Mop to soften the color onto the highlight areas.

2. The pony's harness is RS shaded with BS. The harness button is BS shaded BU.

3. His cheek and hearts are CRS plus a tad of BS highlighted with White.

4. His mane is swirled with BS then BU. Allow base coats to dry.

5. All stitches and liner work are BU. Checks on his legs are White. He has a Black eye with a blue iris and White highlights. There is a little White highlight on his cheek.

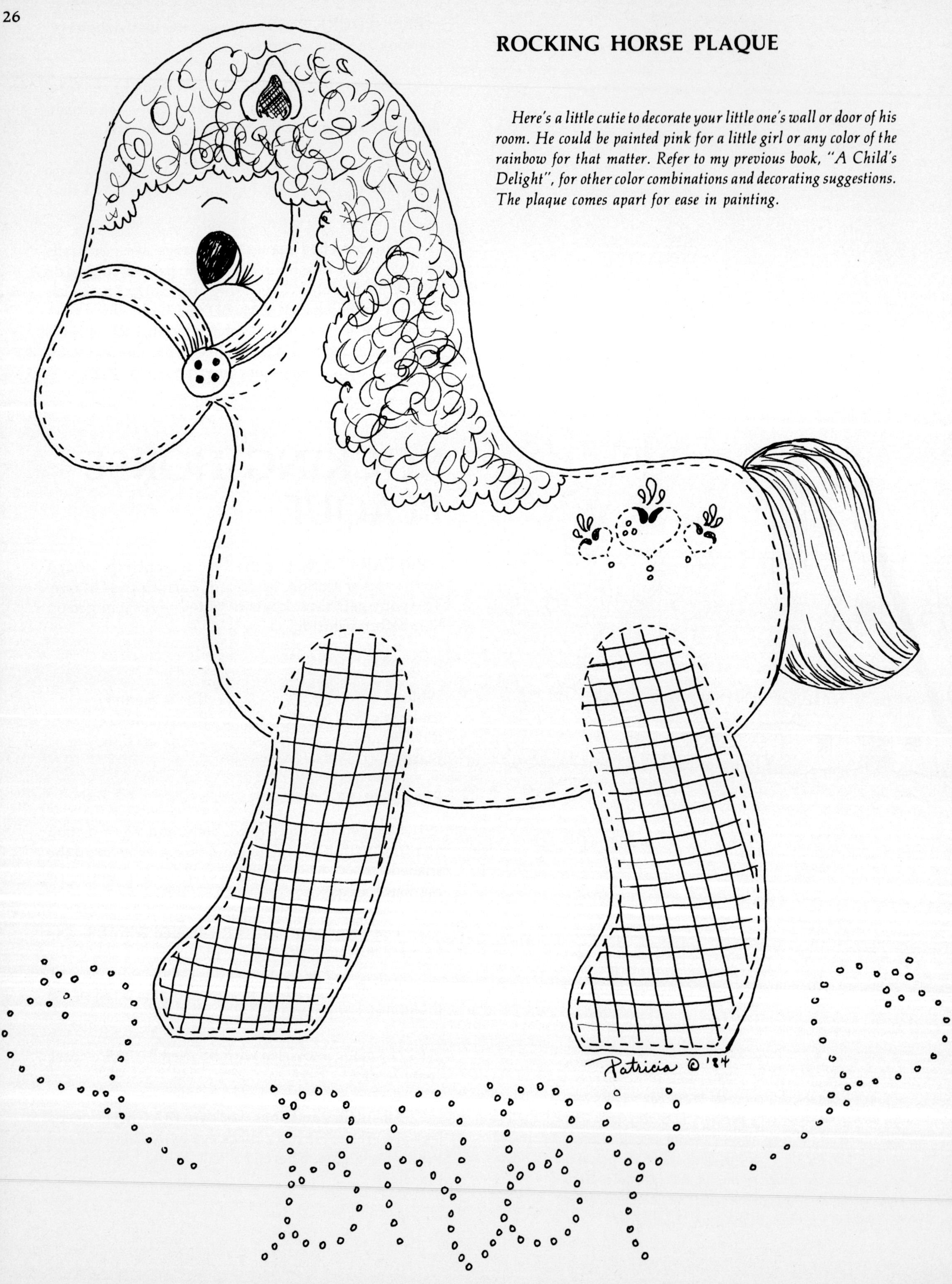

ROCKING HORSE PLAQUE

Here's a little cutie to decorate your little one's wall or door of his room. He could be painted pink for a little girl or any color of the rainbow for that matter. Refer to my previous book, "A Child's Delight", for other color combinations and decorating suggestions. The plaque comes apart for ease in painting.

FIREPLACE BELLOWS

PREPARATION. Use the S931 to punch the hobnail border on the bellows front and the trailing scrolls down the handle. Sand and seal the piece. Stain and allow to dry.

COLORS

White	Raw Sienna
Cadmium Yellow Medium	Burnt Sienna
Yellow Ochre	Burnt Umber
Black	

MIXES

1. Equal parts Cadmium Yellow Medium and Yellow Ochre
2. Mix #1 plus Black (leaf green)

PROCEDURE. Refer to the general instructions for Quilted Applique on Sealed Wood and paint as follows:

1. The tulip center, side polliwogs and base are based in with mix #1, shaded with Raw Sienna and highlighted with mix #1 plus White.

2. The side petals of the tulip are based in Burnt Sienna, shaded with Burnt Umber and highlighted with mix #1.

3. The large polliwogs are based in with #2 mix, shaded with a darker value of mix #2 made by adding a little more Black, and highlighted with White plus mix #1.

4. Allow the based areas to dry. Accent strokes, stitches and dots are Burnt Umber. The tulip center has checks of mix #1.

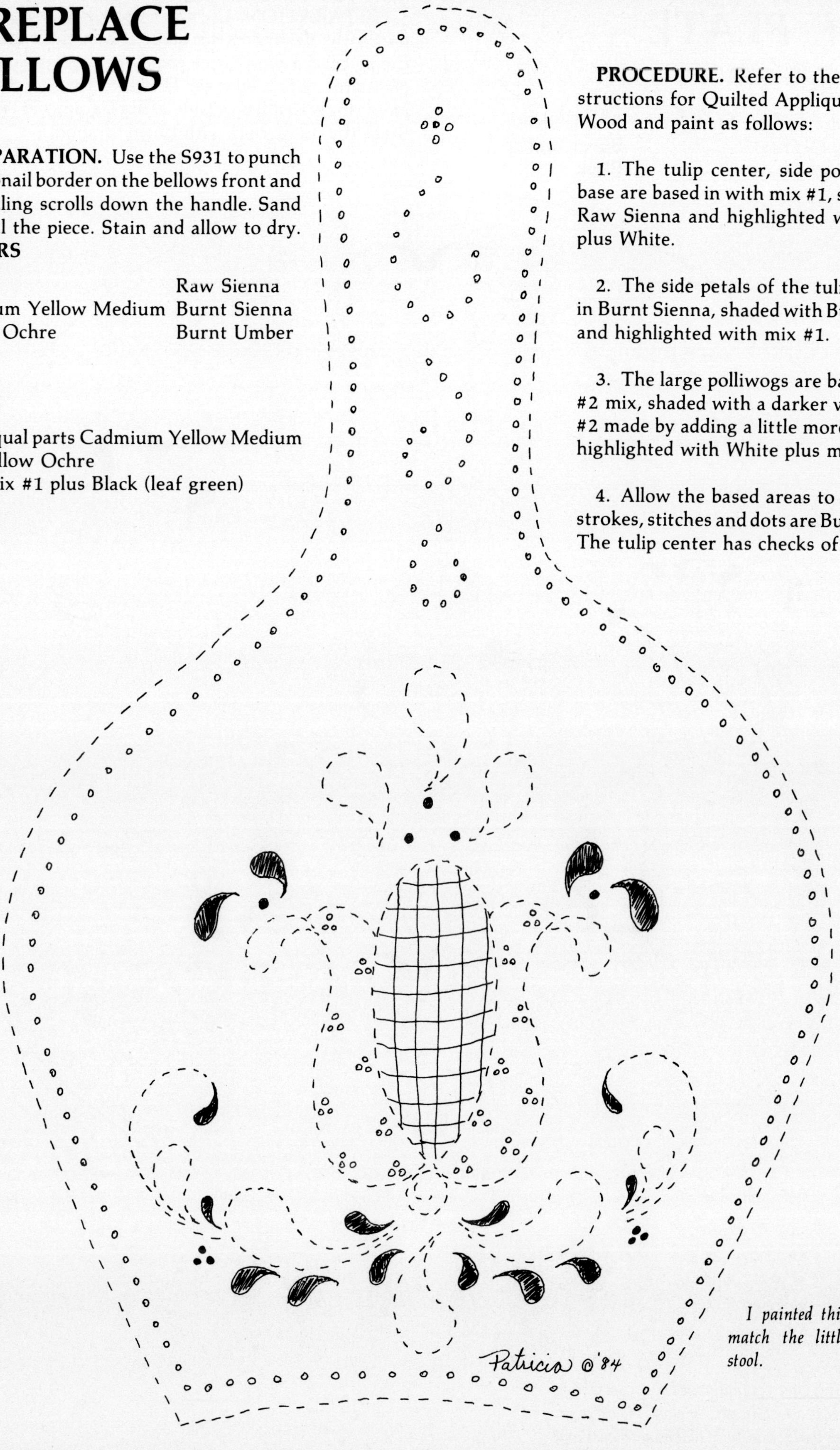

I painted this piece to match the little fireside stool.

Patricia © '84

ALE PLATE

COLORS

Cadmium Yellow Medium
Yellow Ochre
Cadmium Orange

Burnt Sienna
Burnt Umber
Black

PREPARATION. Use the S931, then the S932 to punch the design on the outer rim of the plate. Seal the piece and apply three coats of tinted gesso to the plate area with a sponge. The color band next to the plate rim is Red Iron Oxide Delta Ceramcoat Acrylic. Stain the outer rims with Burnt Umber.

This decorative plate is usually used by artists who do rosemaling as it is a traditional ale plate. However, in this case it lends itself beautifully to the punchwork and quilted applique design.

MIXES

1. Equal parts of Cadmium Yellow Medium and Yellow Ochre
2. #1 mix plus a tad of Black (leaf green)
3. Cadmium Orange plus tads of #1 mix and Burnt Sienna

PROCEDURE. Refer to the general instructions for Quilted Applique on Gessoed Backgrounds and base in the following areas:

1. The bird's head, body, topknot and one tail feather are based in the yellow mix (#1). The cheek is BS. The tulips and the bird's wing, beak, and two tail feathers are orange mix (#3).

2. All of the hearts are BS. All of the foliage polliwogs are leaf green mix (#2).

After the base washes are dry, dampen the entire plate area with "half and half" and float Yellow Ochre around the edges. Use a large mop brush to soften this glaze and fade it out towards the center of the plate. Wipe the glaze off of the individual sections of the design so the highlights are cleared. Allow this to dry.

The stitches, liner work and french knots are BU. The bird has a Black eye that is highlighted with White. The cheek has a White highlight also. The bird's checks are #1 mix and the tulips and remainder of the bird have checks of #3 mix. The Red Iron Oxide band is antiqued with BU and the entire plate area is spattered with BU acrylic for a homespun effect.

CHECKERBOARD

PREPARATION. Use the S931 for the checker board border, the triple dot clusters in the corners and the flower centers on every other square. Use the A99 for all of the little petals. Sand and seal the piece. Dry. Stain the edges with Burnt Umber.

COLORS

White	Raw Sienna
Cadmium Yellow Medium	Burnt Umber
Yellow Ochre	Burnt Sienna
Cadmium Orange	Black

MIXES

1. Equal parts Cadmium Yellow Medium and Yellow Ochre
2. Yellow mix #1 plus a tad of Black (leaf green)
3. Cadmium Orange plus a tad of mix #1

PROCEDURE. Refer to the general instructions for Quilted Applique on Sealed Wood and paint as follows:

1. Every other checkerboard square and the tulip centers and tops are based with mix #1, shaded with Raw Sienna and highlighted with White plus mix #1.

2. The remainder of the checkerboard squares and all of the large polliwogs are based in mix #2, shaded with a darker value of this same mix made by adding a little more Black and highlighted with White plux mix #1.

3. The tulip petals are based with mix #3, shaded with Burnt Sienna and highlighted with mix #1 plus White.

4. Allow the based areas to dry. Accent strokes, stitches and dots are Burnt Umber. The orange tulip petals have checks of mix #3.

SILVERWARE TOTE

PREPARATION. Use the S931 to punch the tatted border and the motifs on the ends of the tote. Sand and seal the piece. Stain and allow to dry.

COLORS

White	Cadmium Red Light
Cadmium Yellow Medium	Cadmium Red Scarlet
Yellow Ochre	Burnt Umber
Cadmium Orange	Burnt Sienna
Black	Raw Sienna

MIXES

1. Equal parts Cadmium Yellow Medium and Yellow Ochre
2. Mix #1 plus Black (leaf green)
3. Cadmium Orange plus a tad of mix #1
4. Cadmium Red Scarlet plus a tad of Burnt Sienna
5. Cadmium Red Light plus Cadmium Red Scarlet (equal parts)

PROCEDURE. Refer to the general instructions for Quilted Applique on Sealed Wood and paint as follows:

1. The heart centers and flower centers are based with mix #5, shaded with mix #4 and highlighted with mix #3.

2. The heart borders and flower petals are based with mix #3, shaded with Raw Sienna, and highlighted with White plus mix #1.

3. The large polliwogs are based in mix #2, shaded with a darker value of mix #2 made by adding a little more Black, and highlighted with White plus mix #1.

4. Allow the based areas to dry. Accent strokes, stitches, dots and rickrack are Burnt Umber. The heart centers have checks of mix #5.

CHECKERBOARD

I remember, as a child, playing a "made up" game using buttons, dice and my grandmother's wedding ring pattern quilt that was on her bed for a playing board. This memory is what gave me the idea for the quilted checkerboard.

Repeat this motif for other half of board